The threefold division of the law

Jonathan Bayes

THE
CHRISTIAN
INSTITUTE

CHRISTIAN INFLUENCE IN A SECULAR WORLD

This article is reprinted from one which first appeared in
Reformation Today Issue 177

First printed in August 2005

ISBN 1 901086 31 - 3

Published by The Christian Institute
PO Box 1, Newcastle upon Tyne, NE7 7EF

Traditional Reformed theology has distinguished God's law revealed in the Old Testament Scriptures into three parts, moral, ceremonial and civil (or judicial). It teaches that the moral element in the law, focused in the ten commandments, is of permanent application, while the ceremonial and civil elements were for the duration of the Old Testament economy only. The ceremonial was a shadow of Christ which became obsolete with his coming, and the civil a model of legal arrangements for any society, though not of such a status as to demand exact replication. My present purpose is to establish whether or not the threefold division is valid. Detailed discussion of the implications in terms of the continuation and abrogation of the respective parts of the law is beyond the scope of this article, though it will be necessary to make occasional reference to the issue.

In the final chapter of *The Institutes* Calvin writes:

> We must attend to the well-known division which distributes the whole law of God, as promulgated by Moses, into the moral, the ceremonial, and the judicial law.[1]

Similarly, Francis Turretin, one of Calvin's successors at Geneva in the middle years of the seventeenth century, has written:

> The law given by Moses is usually distinguished into three species: moral (treating of morals or of perpetual duties towards God and our neighbour); ceremonial (of the ceremonies or rites about the sacred things to be observed under the Old Testament); and civil (constituting the civil government of the Israelite people).[2]

Two years after Turretin's death the *1689 Baptist Confession* incorporated reference to this threefold division of the law. Chapter 19 of the Confession was entitled *Of the Law of God*. It was taken over with only minor modifications from the Westminster Confession of 1646, which represents the distilled essence of Puritan theology. While recognising the primacy of the moral law, the Puritan confessions speak also of the ceremonial laws governing the worship of the people of Israel and prefiguring Christ, and the judicial laws governing the political life of Israel.

Although the threefold division of the law is associated with Reformed theology, and has even been described as 'the cornerstone of Reformed orthodoxy', it would be a mistake to assume that these distinctions were novelties at the time of the Reformation. Turretin notes that the threefold division is 'usual'. Calvin speaks of 'the well known division'. I J Hesselink traces this division back to the medieval scholastic theologian, Thomas Aquinas.[3] It was around 1270 that Aquinas wrote:

> We must therefore distinguish three kinds of precept in the Old Law; viz. 'moral' precepts, which are dictated by the natural law; 'ceremonial' precepts, which are determinations of the Divine worship; and 'judicial' precepts, which are determinations of the justice to be maintained among men.[4]

Despite Hesselink's claim that this threefold division originated with Aquinas, it seems *prima facie* probable that the idea (even if not the precise terminology) has a longer pedigree. Calvin refers to 'the ancients who adopted this division'. Such a turn of phrase suggests that he was looking back further than the thirteenth century.[5]

In his *Summa Theologica* Aquinas refers frequently to Augustine. Distinctions within the law were already familiar by the time of this fifth-century theologian, although he operates with a twofold rather than a threefold division. In AD 400 Augustine wrote a reply to a Manichaean attack on the Old Testament. In the course of this work Augustine introduces a distinction between the moral and the symbolical precepts of the law:

> For example, 'Thou shalt not covet' is a moral precept; 'Thou shalt circumcise every male on the eighth day' is a symbolical precept.[6]

By 'symbolical' precepts Augustine clearly means what would later become known as the ceremonial law; he seems to have given little consideration to the civil law.

However, we can trace these distinctions even further back than the fifth century. At this early stage in the development of Christian theology the distinctions within the law are not fully worked out, but they are clearly implicit. Writing about two hundred years before Augustine, Tertullian distinguishes what he terms 'the primordial law' or 'the natural law' from 'the sacerdotal law' or 'the Levitical law'.[7] At one point Tertullian seems to recognise the difference between what would later come to be known as the moral and civil parts of the law when he distinguishes the 'prime counsels of innocence, chastity, and justice, and piety' from the 'prescriptions of humanity'.[8]

However, the threefold division can be found already in the period earlier than Tertullian. In the mid-second century Ptolemaeus, a gnostic heretic, found three sections to God's law. Johannes Quasten explains:

> The first section contains the pure law, untainted by evil, in other words the ten commandments. This is the section of the Mosaic law which Jesus came to fulfil rather than to suspend. The second section is the law adulterated with injustice, namely that of retaliation, which was suspended by the Saviour. The third section is the ceremonial law which the Saviour spiritualised.[9]

According to Jean Daniélou, the reason why Ptolemaeus regarded the second part of the law as a mixture of good and bad was that it was 'the result of adaptation to circumstances'.[10]

However, it would be a mistake to treat the idea of the threefold division of the law as suspect on the assumption that it originated with a heretic. Daniélou points out that the orthodox Justin Martyr, who wrote around the same time as Ptolemaeus, also suggested a threefold division in his *Dialogue with Trypho, a Jew*:

> Justin too distinguishes three types of material in the Law, 'one which was ordained for piety and the practice of righteousness', and another which was instituted 'either to be a mystery of the Messiah or because of the hardness of heart of your people'.[11]

One of the most primitive post-apostolic writers whose work is still extant, the early second-century Barnabas, also recognised the need for distinctions within God's law. He notes that sacrifices, burnt offerings and oblations have been abolished and replaced by 'the new law of our Lord Jesus Christ', as has circumcision. However, he is clear that believers must 'utterly flee from all the works of lawlessness', and in spelling out 'The Way of Light' which Christians must walk in contrast with 'The Way of the Black One', he quotes most of the ten commandments and insists, 'You shall not desert the commandments of the Lord.'[12] Clearly, Barnabas, at this early stage of Christian theological development, was already feeling the need for distinctions within the law of God.

Sometimes, as is common in patristic literature, he uses the word 'law' as functionally equivalent to 'covenant', and so distinguishes the old law, which is completely abrogated, with the new law revealed in Jesus Christ. However, at other times he uses the vocabulary of law more specifically of the sacrificial system or of the moral demands of the faith. In this more specific sense, the law is abolished only in certain parts: the sacrificial system has gone, but moral demand remains.

Moreover, the threefold division of the law is not only a Christian construct. Judaism also recognises that there are distinctions to be made. The mid-twentieth century Jewish writer, Boaz Cohen, notes that the divine law consists 'of ceremonialism, jurisprudence and ethics', and finds this threefold division indicated in the words 'commandment' (*mizvah*), 'statutes' (*hoqim*) and 'judgements' (*mispatim*) in

Deuteronomy 6:1, and in verse 20, where 'commandment' is replaced by 'testimonies' (*edah*). Cohen's terms are recognisably equivalent to the traditional Christian vocabulary. Moreover, Cohen, like the Christian Reformed tradition, describes the Decalogue as moral principles.[13]

Samuel Holdheim was a nineteenth-century German rabbi. He too distinguished at least between the moral and the ritual parts of the law. Ralph Bisschops notes that Holdheim saw the destruction of the temple in AD 70 as God's declaration that 'sacrificing animals could no longer be held as true worship'. Bisschops explains:

> The observation of the moral laws laid down in Mosaic Revelation is an unconditional obligation for every Jew. Holdheim defines the moral laws as those laws which are eternally true and not bound to the particular mentality of the Jews at the time of Moses. As to the ritual laws, their purpose is to stimulate devotion ... According to Holdheim, the ritual laws are to be regarded as mere "crutches", helping man to develop deep inner devotion. They are the form of Jewish religion, whereas ethics are its substance. They make up the outer appearance, whereas ethics constitutes the core.[14]

Amongst contemporary Jews, there are those who recognise that it is simply impracticable to observe all the laws in the circumstances of the modern world:

> A large portion of the laws relate to sacrifices and offerings, which can only he made in the Temple, and the Temple does not exist today. Some of the laws relate to the theocratic state of Israel, its king, its supreme court, and its system of justice, and cannot be observed because the theocratic state of Israel does not exist today.[15]

This categorisation of those laws which cannot still be practised tallies very closely with the two parts of the law which have become known in Christian parlance as the ceremonial and the civil law respectively, and which traditional Christian theology has seen as superseded.

In spite of this impressive pedigree of the threefold division of the law, there have been those who have questioned its validity. One such is John Metcalfe, who, in his typical colourful style, writes:

> What! rend asunder the one law of God into three mutilated parts, inventing the names moral, judicial, and ceremonial, just so that you can discard two and retain one? But what God has joined together, let not man put asunder. The law, one law, as such, was given by Moses. Then either we are under it, or we are not under it. It is impossible for anyone to be under only a part of it. ... God called the whole, *the law*. Israel calls it *the law*. And so did Paul, agreeing with Israel, the Jews, and the Lord Jesus, none of whom allowed of this dismemberment. It is *the law*, integrally, the whole of it, all that Moses commanded, and none of it can be separated from any other part of it.[16]

Another representative of this school of thought, at least to some extent, is Edgar Andrews, whose recent commentary on Galatians proceeds on the assumption that,

> There is no indication in Galatians that Paul ever thinks of the law as being divided into different parts (moral, civil, ceremonial).

Rather,

> Paul sees the law as indivisible. ... There is no evidence that Paul ever thought of the law as being divided into separate parts; he speaks explicitly about 'the whole law'.[17]

Nevertheless, it is necessary to add some qualifications when considering Andrews' position. Despite this insistence on the essential unity of the law, he does suggest that a two-part analysis can be made:

> In the first part (or aspect), we see what a holy God required of his people, and what penalties were applied to those in Israel who broke his commandments. In the second aspect we see the provision God made for the forgiveness and reconciliation of those who sinned. This second aspect prefigured the work of Christ.[18]

Andrews works with a twofold division by conflating the moral law and the civil law, arguing that the 'civil law' is really an amplification of the ten commandments. This point is not altogether without substance: the civil law was indeed the application to Israelite society of the moral principles enshrined in the Decalogue. Nevertheless, it is as well to retain the distinction between the absolute principles and their application in the context of specific social arrangements, In any case, it is evident that Andrews acknowledges that this aspect of the law is distinguishable from what is usually termed the 'ceremonial law'.

As a matter of fact, it is virtually impossible to carry through a rigorous rejection of the threefold (or at least a twofold) division. Andrews says:

> Those who are Spirit-led will fulfil the righteous requirements of the law. … But this will not be because they subject themselves to the law, but because they are guided by the indwelling Spirit.[19]

It is clear that the phrase 'the righteous requirements of the law' is not intended to include the requirements of the laws to do with sacrifice, circumcision, diet, and the like. Andrews implicitly recognises that there is a section of the law (described as 'righteous requirements'), which can be distinguished from other parts of the law, and which remains the definitive expression of the Spirit-led life. The phrase 'moral law' has been replaced by the phrase 'righteous requirements of the law', but the two appear to be identical in content. Thus, despite the assertion that the law is indivisible, those who deny the threefold division cannot avoid making distinctions by default, even though they may reject the traditional terminology, and even though they prefer to speak of 'aspects' rather than 'parts' of the law.

However, it is time to turn to the all-important question: does Scripture affirm a threefold division of the law? Whatever commentators, Jewish or Christian, might say, the issue hangs on the teaching of the Word of God. Those involved in the debate, from both sides, are committed to the authority and inerrancy of the Bible. Their discussion concerns the proper interpretation of the Scriptures.

My purpose is to demonstrate that the Word of God does indeed uphold the threefold division of the law, and that the traditional Reformed classification is correct. It follows that the implications of this division are also correct: the ceremonial and civil law are abrogated, but the moral law remains in force for all time as the declaration of divinely ordained ethical principles and as the rule of life for the true believer, who will inevitably 'delight in the law of God according to the inward man' (Rom 7:22). The exposition of these implications is, however, beyond the scope of this article.

We take as our starting point the words of Samuel to Saul in I Samuel 15:22:

> Has the LORD as *great* delight in burnt offerings and sacrifices as in obeying the voice of the LORD? Behold, to obey is better than sacrifice, and to heed than the fat of rams.

These words are echoed by Hosea 6:6, where God protests:

> I desire mercy and not sacrifice, and the knowledge of God more than burnt offerings,

The same sentiment appears also in Proverbs 21:3:

> To do righteousness and justice is more acceptable to the LORD than sacrifice.

Such verses give the lie to Jakob Jocz's assertion that 'the division between the strictly moral and the 'ceremonial' in our sense was entirely unknown to the Jews'.[20] Here are affirmations both of the distinction between the moral and the ceremonial law and of the primacy of the former. The Proverbs text, with its dual reference to 'righteousness and justice' probably indicates the further analysis of the former part of the law into both strictly moral and civil components. These verses also teach the primacy of the moral law and its civil application over the ceremonial. This was a theme which was to become dominant in the writings of the prophets. Alec Motyer summarises the prophetic message as follows:

> The nation has missed the divine priority by its concentration on the mere operation of a cult, for the cult is not a thing which exists on its own but rather for the sake of the spiritual needs of a people committed to the moral law of God.[21]

This prophetic concern may be illustrated by reference to a number of passages. In Isaiah 1:11-17 God denounces the sacrifices as purposeless. He has had enough of them, and finds no delight in them. The reason is the uncleanness of the people. The solution to the distastefulness of the sacrificial ritual is not its abolition, but rather that the people should:

> Cease to do evil, learn to do good; seek justice, reprove the oppressor; defend the fatherless, plead for the widow.

Fastidiousness in ceremonial observation is invalidated unless it goes hand-in-hand with obedience to the moral law and its social application in the civil law.

Later, in Isaiah 43:22-24, we find God complaining that it is not to Him that Israel has brought its numerous sacrifices; He has remained unsatisfied. The reason is that their sins have become a wearisome burden to the Lord. The words 'sins' and 'iniquities' used in verse 24 clearly have moral and social connotations in this context, where compliance with the LORD's ceremonial requirements alone is insufficient to count as obedience to the law.

In similar vein, Jeremiah 6:19-20 gives God's pronouncement of impending calamity on the people 'because they have not heeded my words, nor my law, but rejected it'. This is not a complaint against a failure in ceremonial observation, because the LORD immediately refers to their burnt offerings and sacrifices. However, their law-breaking makes these unacceptable. Clearly here, 'law' refers to ethical demand in distinction from the ritual requirements, which have been carefully followed: 'Ritual performances divorced from a proper moral attitude are worthless in God's sight.'[22]

Amos, too, takes up this theme:

> Though you offer me burnt offerings and your grain offerings, I will not
> accept *them*, nor will I regard your fattened peace offerings.

The word 'fattened' seems designed to highlight the people's ardour in observance of these ceremonial requirements. However, they are of no avail, because justice and righteousness are missing (Amos 5:22-24). God's moral requirements, and their application to civil society, are paramount. Micah 6:6-8 makes the same point:

> To a generation preoccupied with things ceremonial to the neglect of
> weightier matters of the law, Micah needs to bring a counterstress on the
> impact of the covenant upon all of life's concerns. ... To keep Yahweh
> confined in a gilded cultic cage was a travesty of faith in a moral God.[23]

Perhaps all this may be summed up by the statement of Proverbs 15:8: 'The sacrifice of the wicked *is* an abomination to the LORD.'

The same emphasis is found in the words of the Psalmist. Psalm 40:6 reads:

> Sacrifice and offering you did not desire; ... burnt offering and sin offering
> you did not require.

The explanation of this apparent rejection of God's ceremonial instructions is that it is the person who delights to do God's will because his law is written in the heart who genuinely fulfils his will. If we must emphasise one or the other, the moral demands of God must always take precedence over the ritual.

When we turn to the New Testament we discover that the same distinctions continue. Our starting point in this instance will be I Corinthians 7:19:

> Circumcision is nothing and uncircumcision is nothing, but keeping the
> commandments of God *is what matters*.

To a Jew this would have seemed a remarkable statement. Circumcision was one of God's foremost commandments: it was commanded by Yahweh as the sign and seal of his covenant. Evidently

Paul could discern distinctions within God's law which set certain commandments apart as applicable to all Christians, while others were irrelevant. This is tantamount to the division between the moral and the ceremonial law.

Similarly, in Romans 2:25-27 the apostle repeatedly contrasts circumcision and law, even though, to the Jew 'circumcision was not something other than law-keeping; on the contrary, it was the most fundamental part of the covenant and its law'.[24] However, Paul is well aware that there are distinctions to be made within the law of God.

Further New Testament evidence for the threefold division is found in passages such as Matthew 5:17-48, Matthew 19:18-19, and Romans 13:9, especially when they are read alongside the many passages, such as the book of Hebrews, which speak of the irrelevance of circumcision and the obsolescence of the Levitical and sacrificial requirements. The commandments which are cited in the New Testament as having convicting power or as God's continuing demands for the believing life are clearly distinguished from those which were specific to the Jews at a certain time. This observation upholds the view that the moral commandments are to be treated separately from those which are suspended, which had a ceremonial purport.

When the Pharisees challenged Jesus over the failure of his disciples to wash their hands, in breach of a rabbinical extension to all the people of the requirements for the priests in Exodus 30:19,21, Jesus side-stepped the issue, and turned instead to the fifth commandment. He evidently had different priorities in legal interpretation from the Pharisees. In other words, his concern was moral where theirs was ceremonial.

In his book *Tablets of Stone* John Reisinger writes:

> The term 'moral law' is a theological term developed in the Middle Ages and is not a biblical term in any sense whatsoever. The term may, or may not, be a correct and useful term if it can be proven to be scripturally correct. However, the term would first have to be established with texts of Scripture that clearly prove the doctrine implied or stated in the term.[25]

Leaving aside the minor point that Reisinger is inaccurate in his dating (we have already seen that the term 'moral law' originated at least as early as Augustine), it must be acknowledged that he speaks truly when he says that it is a term which is not found as such in the Bible. However, I am confident that the texts of Scripture to which reference has here been made do establish that the idea contained in the term is biblical. Although the words 'moral', 'civil', and 'ceremonial' are theological, it is apparent that they do justice to vital scriptural distinctions. 'These theological designations collect important biblical teachings into brief phrases.'[26] The threefold division of the law is indeed taught in the Word of God.

This article is reprinted from one which first appeared in *Reformation Today* Issue 177

References

[1] Calvin, J, *Institutes of the Christian Religion*, Translated by Henry Beveridge, James Clark & Co., 1962, Volume 2, Book 4, Chapter 20, Section 14, page 663

[2] Turretin, F, *Institutes of Elenctic Theology*, 11.24.1

[3] Hesselink I J, *Calvin's Concept of the Law*, Pickwick, 1992, page 102

[4] Thomas Aquinas, *Summa Theologica, 2a, Question 99, Article 4*

[5] Calvin J, *Op cit*, Volume 2, Book 4, Chapter 20, Section 14

[6] Augustine, *Contra Faustum Manichaeum*, 6.2

[7] Tertullian, *An Answer to the Jews*, chapters 2 and 5

[8] Tertullian, *Five Books Against Marcion*, 2.17

[9] Quasten, J, *Patrology*, Volume 1, Christian Classics, 1984, page 261

[10] Daniélou, J, *Gospel Message and Hellenistic Culture*, Darton, Longman and Todd, 1973, page 222

[11] *Ibid*, page 223

[12] The Epistle of Barnabas, chapters 2, 4, and 19, see *The Apostolic Fathers, Volume 1: Translated by Kirsopp Lake*, Harvard University Press, 1998, pages 341-409

[13] Cohen, B, *Law and Tradition in Judaism*, The Jewish Theological Seminary of America, 1959, pages 188-189

[14] Bisschops R, 'Metaphor as the Internalisation of a Ritual. With a Case Study on Samuel Holdheim (1806-1860)', in Francis, J and Bisschops, R (Eds.), *Metaphor, Canon, and Community: Jewish, Christian and Islamic Approaches*, Religions and Discourse, 1,1999, page 291

[15] Rich, T R, *Judaism 101*, see section *What does Halakhah Consist of? see http://*www.jewfaq.org as at 12 July 2005

[16] Metcalfe, J, *Deliverance From the Law: The Westminster Confession Exploded*, John Metcalfe Publishing Trust, 1992, pages 5 and 8

[17] Andrews E H, *Free in Christ: The Message of Galatians*, Evangelical Press, 1996, page 86

[18] *Ibid*, page 89

[19] *Ibid*, page 293

[20] Jocz, J, *The Jewish People and Jesus Christ: The Relationship Between Church and Synagogue*, Baker Book House, 1949, page 68

[21] Motyer, J A, 'Prophecy, Prophets', in Douglas, J D (Ed.), *The Illustrated Bible Dictionary, Part 3*, IVP, 1980, page 1284

[22] Thompson, J A, *The Book of Jeremiah*, Eerdmans Publishing Company, 1980, page 262

[23] Allen, L C, *The Books of Joel, Obadiah, Jonah and Micah*, Eerdmans Publishing Company, 1976, pages 374-375

[24] Dunn, J D G, *Romans 1-8: Word Biblical Commentary*, Word Books, 1988, page 126

[25] Reisinger, J G, *Tablets of Stone*, Crowne Publications, 1989, page 14

[26] Chantry, W, *God's Righteous Kingdom*, Banner of Truth, 1980, page 113

The threefold division of the law